UNCONDITIONAL
LOVE
God's Love For His
Fallen Creatures

Copyright page

Publisher's Name: Rose Atkins

ISBN: 978-1-962142-21-2

Contents

INTRODUCTION 1

CHAPTER 1 3
CHILDHOOD

CHAPTER 2 7
THE SCHOOL YEARS

CHAPTER 3 11
BECOMING A WIFE

CHAPTER 4 17
SUBMITTING TO CHRIST

CHAPTER 5...21
DREAMS AND CHANGE

CHAPTER 6 33
MARRIAGE

CHAPTER 7...39
THE WOLF IN SHEEP'S CLOTHING

CHAPTER 8 51
MY RESTORATION

CHAPTER 9 55
A NEW LOVE

CHAPTER 10 59
SECOND CALL TO AFRICA

CHAPTER 11 79
VOLCANIC ERUPTION

CHAPTER 12...93
NEPAL BY DIVINE APPOINTMENT

ABOUT THE AUTHOR 95

Contents

INTRODUCTION

The heart of God overflows with love for His children. He loves us so much that He gave His best! He gave His one and only Son as a ransom for His fallen creatures. We have been born into a world of sin and destined for eternal destruction. Our Heavenly Father desires to shower us with His blessings and love. His goal is to restore fallen humanity into His image so that we can become a reflection of Him.

The process can be painful, but the result can be His masterpiece as we give to Him! My life's story is a classic example of His handiwork, guided by His unconditional love. He transformed a lost soul into a vessel fit for His use! This testimony is in the sequence of its occurrence. I pray our Heavenly Father blesses you as you read and see how He unveils His excellent, loving, Fatherly guidance and intervention in my life.

CHAPTER 1

CHILDHOOD

I remember watching with envy in preschool as fathers played with their children. The children were so happy, jumping, laughing, and playing with their dads. These moments always gave me a deep feeling of emptiness, lack, and envy because I did not have a father. My dad had left us while we were babies, causing a lack of love and nurture in my life. The absence of a father image left a void in me.

I remember one incident when I was around three or four years old, sitting about four steps high on the porch. My mom had married an army soldier. They might have been arguing. He came out of the house in such a rage. I was sitting at the top of the steps; he had on his Military boots and kicked me like a football off the top step! I landed on the ground and am unable to remember anything else. That was my experience with my father.

PEARL HARBOR ATTACK THROUGH THE EYES OF A CHILD

We lived in Kahili, Oahu, Hawaii, blocks away and across from Hickam Air Force Base. Pearl Harbor was close by. I was around seven years of age when the attack on Pearl Harbor occurred. I can clearly remember and visualize the air combat in the sky above the Military installation. Although I cannot recall all the occurrences, I will share the bits and pieces to the best of my recollection.

I recall running after my mother, who was in a state of panic, running with the crowds of locals on Nimitz Highway, Honolulu, Oahu. Sirens were wailing; I still, to this day, get flashbacks whenever I hear a siren! My little legs could barely keep up with her as I stayed close behind her in terror. Above us, the Japanese planes were firing the guns at their targets, Hickam Air Force Base. Pearl Harbor was just next to Hickam. It looked as though flames were coming out from the guns that were firing in the skies above from the Japanese planes. I have no memory of where we were running or where we ended up, but I never stopped until we got there.

After these events, I recollect us kids and adults huddled around the radio, listening to the announcements broadcast to the residents. My Grandfather turned off the lights at my grandparents' home in Kaneohe, Oahu. The radio announced the news and was covered with cloth to keep the light from shining. There was a fear that the enemy would detect the lights and that we all might be prisoners. We moved about in the darkness. I am trying to remember how we ended up in Kaneohe from Nimitz Highway, but that is the sequence of events.

We eventually returned to school as the danger subsided. However, the terror still lingered. At school, a soldier fitted us with gas masks in a gas chamber and checked our masks for leaks. The gas masks issued by the military were in an olive-colored canvas bag shaped like a miniature ham with a strap that hung over our shoulders. Each student carried a gas mask as part of our daily routine. Our teachers conducted drills daily and instructed us to march a single file from the classroom to the back of the building so we could huddle in trenches for safety in case of attack.

We took shortcuts on our daily walk to school to shorten the distance. Walking through the trees and brush, we met foxholes with camouflage covering the soldiers who ran the massive guns (cannons) protruding and facing in our direction. The soldiers were still and did not come out of their foxholes as we walked before their guns (cannon). They acted like they did not see us, and we acted like we didn't notice them as we continued our walk.

I can remember the food and gasoline shortages that occurred. Food, other staples, and gasoline became unavailable to the Hawaiian Islands without obtaining a rationing card or certificate. Then, long lines formed to receive the items. I am unsure of the method used as my mother had access. Toilet tissue was scarce, and so were other paper products. We mostly ate poi taro as rice and other products were unavailable. These events affected many lives.

Finally, things returned to normal, and we continued with our lives!

TESTIMONIES FROM FAMILY MEMBERS OF THE ATTACK

Some of my family members were civilian employees during the incident. Thank God it happened on a Sunday when they were not at work!

My Father, Francisco "Frank" Padilla, was a civilian employee at Pearl Harbor. When we later met him as adults, I was aware of his involvement in recovering bodies and rescuing sailors from the ships in the Harbor. His superiors gave him a letter of commendation for his participation, but the letter vanished over the years.

My uncle, James Ocasio Torres, my mother's brother, was a plumber at Pearl Harbor. He worked on board docked ships. His wife, Annie Santos Torres, was a secretary at Hickam Air Force Base. She would tell us stories of the bullet holes in the walls of the hangar in which she worked.

Other members of the family joined the military or were federally employed.

I thank God He kept my family safe.

CHAPTER 2
THE SCHOOL YEARS

The Lord has used dreams often in my life. I had a vivid dream in which I drowned! I was immersed in the blue ocean and surrounded by many bubbles floating around me. Yes, my dream was in color! From bubbly blue water, I saw the water turn red like blood! I looked ahead and saw a figure dressed in a white tunic with both arms stretched towards me.

It was not until years later, when I became more familiar with the Bible, that I learned of the shed blood of Jesus and the blood covering for sin and protection.

Sometime after this dream, when I was around twelve years old, I did have an experience of drowning. The sand bar dropped significantly during a Girl Scout outing to Sand Island on Oahu, and I fell into it. A lifeguard who went with us on our excursion rescued and resuscitated me!

There are multiple references to dreams available in the Bible! That could also be called a warning!

I graduated from St Anne's Elementary School, and the Catholic Church provided a scholarship —a blessing from the Lord! Another scholarship was available for my high school education, but I would have to travel from Kaneohe, Oahu, to Honolulu. My Mom declined the offer, saying it would be too far for me to travel, so I ended up in public school at Castle High School in Kaneohe, Oahu.

The nuns taught me proper English, as I could only speak pidgin English; Spanish was the language spoken at home. They also instructed me to wear shoes as I was in the habit of running barefoot like all the local children. Our dress code required us to wear uniforms. I had morals and religion formed early in my life to love, honor, and obey God and His Commandments! I loved Jesus so much; He was my constant companion! I decided to become a nun and serve God at an early age.

"For ye have not received the spirit of bondage again to fear; but ye have received the Spirit of adoption, whereby we cry, Abba, Father. The Spirit itself bearish witness with our spirit that we are the children of God:" Romans 8:15-16 (KJV)

The above scripture freed me from the bondage of emptiness and the lack of a father in my life. The realization stunned me and made me understand what I had read; I was unaware of it! Although my earthly father was absent, I always had a father who loved and cared for me. Praise Abba, my Father God!

MY TEEN YEARS

Upon entering public school, my vision of life changed! I had been wearing dresses to school, and the other girls wore jeans. Here, my life took a turn, and I started to change just to fit in. The girls made fun of me because I was different, and a girl provoked me. I had no problem with the boys. One of the girls kept coming alongside me and would deliberately bang or push me! She was jealous as one of the football players she liked had invited me to his senior prom and gave me his letter.

She persisted until I got upset and challenged me to a fight! I would not back down to her challenge, so I agreed to meet her after school. After school, I was fuming mad and marched home to change from my dress into my jeans. I made a colossal mistake wearing a shirt with buttons. When I arrived at the school, the kids had already formed a human ring, and she was in the center of it, waiting for me. We fought physically, rough and tumble, while the kids cheered us on. My shirt had pulled open as I had lost all the buttons. Then, out of nowhere, the sports coach intervened, broke up the fight, and scheduled an appointment to speak to us individually. During my visit to his office, all I remember him saying was, "I know who started it."

 I was released. Later, I discovered that my opponent had taken karate lessons! My life changed from being proper to self-preservation.

Ninth grade was a challenge and adjustment for me as I learned to adjust my life to my surroundings after my first initiation and introduction to real life. I started to enjoy high school! My sophomore, junior, and senior years were a blast! Football games, friends, school dances, and so much more!

My High School Photo

I took a summer job working at Dole Cannery in Honolulu as a trimmer. I was the person who trimmed the pineapples for canning— to buy school clothes. Wearing my fashionable outfits to school each year gained me the honor of being voted *Best Dressed*. By then, I had become one of the most popular girls in school. I also enjoyed the benefits of being voted Princess of Oahu for our May Day Program for three years in high school, which was important! I experienced Hawaii's pomp and pageantry, Hawaiian music, hula dancing, Royal Court, excitement, and beauty!

As the Princess of Oahu, I enjoyed wearing my beautiful holoku. Haku crown, and Ilima leis. This traditional outfit for Hawaiian celebrations is a holoku, a woman's long one-piece gown usually made fitted with a train and worn, especially in Hawaii. A haku is a crown made of fresh flowers. My holoku and flowers were pale orange, the color of the sunshine. I felt wonderful. There was so much excitement as the faculty, students, and families took it all in. It was such a festive and regal event!

I did very well in my classes, scoring an A or B. I suppose this was all thanks to my ridged Catholic training. LOL!

Oh yes, another crucial part of those teenage years—boys! Hum, they were fascinating! The top football and basketball players usually invited me to school functions and on dates; I enjoyed the attention and honor of being seen with the most popular boys.

During my junior year of high school, I met my future husband, who excelled in basketball and was considered a catch. At that time, I did not know he would pursue and aggressively keep other boys from approaching me in any way with threats.

CHAPTER 3
BECOMING A WIFE

Before continuing, I wish to clarify that whatever I share here is to give God the glory for His powerful intervention in my life. He not only saved me spiritually but also intervened when I helplessly looked to end my life and no longer wanted to live in this world! Whatever happened, including what I mentioned in this chapter, is forgiven and placed under the blood covering of my Savior! No one is perfect except for Jesus, God's only Son! To Him be all the glory and honor forever and ever! Amen.

MY FIRST MARRIAGE

My future husband was a senior when I was a junior in high school. I had not heard from or seen him during my final year of high school. I graduated high school, took the nursing exam, and passed it. And I was accepted into the Nursing Program. Somehow, he discovered where I was and started calling regularly at the dorm. Then he started visiting me at the dorm! I did not discourage him as I liked him and was flattered by his attention. But things soon took a wrong turn.

One day, while I was visiting outside in the lanai area, with another male visitor from high school who popped in suddenly to see me, guess who came walking in? Yep, my future husband! We had no plans then, but I assume he felt he had rights. So, he went into a rage, cussed my friend out, then told him to leave and never come back! I was stunned and afraid. That was a red flag to which I should have paid attention, but in my ignorance, I took it as his expression of love for me! I did not know the difference. Because of the abuse I had experienced in my childhood, I considered this normal behavior. All I knew of love was what I had read in fairy tales. Girl meets Prince Charming, he kisses her, and they live happily ever after!

What a joke! Hello! Because I ignored the signs when he proposed, we got married. Little did I know what I had just committed myself to.

I left nursing school, took courses to complete my nursing career, took the exams, and became an LPN in Hawaii.

THE ABUSE

I won't go into the sordid details and drag out this testimony except to recap some of my ordeals. I plan to focus on the Spiritual aspects of my deliverance by a loving, wonderful Father who is involved, protects, and cares for His children.

During this marriage, I experienced physical abuse of all sorts. My husband's fists conducted most of the abuse. I had received punches all over my body, including to the abdomen, while I was pregnant. There were times I had such severe bruising that the emergency room physician called the police. My neck, my legs, it didn't matter. I'd walk into the emergency room with blood gushing down from my nostrils from being punched in the face or, in another instance, be unable to walk from a baseball-sized bruise to the right thigh. He punched me repeatedly as though I was a punching bag into a shower door so hard it shattered with me going through it. Besides the physical abuse, abandonment, silent treatments, and loneliness, he never wanted to be seen with the children and me, concealing the fact that he was married, in public always to spend time away from home with friends, drinking, gambling, completely detached as though he was single. Disappearing for days without me knowing where he was or when he would return home, I worried that he might have been in an accident or that something terrible had happened to him. My concerns brought on anxiety, which then turned into anger when I discovered he was out having a good time, having gambled away his paycheck. In one episode, after being beaten and severely bruised, I walked to the police station; we lived across from the police station. I tried to file a complaint, and the police told me they could not act since he was in the military; it was out of their hands. Another time, the military emergency room physician recommended that if I filed charges, he would lose his rank, and our paycheck would decrease. It just seemed like a hopeless situation. Our children were infants, and I needed the extra money for expenses. There were little to no available services for domestic emergency aid in those days.

When I expressed my feelings of wanting him to spend holidays or time with us, he would become violent and would attack me; he was never available. I must admit he was a good provider and felt that was the only thing necessary to be a husband or father. I was forbidden to hold and cuddle my children. He would become angry and say that I was going to spoil them. Removing my crying baby from my arms and tossing her into her crib caused a bounce while I watched helplessly, knowing that if I responded in any way, I would be next. Discipline was his main concern always. I could not receive help from the Church or police when I sought help. During this period of emotional detachment, I discovered my escape in Jesus. He became my confidence, He met my emotional needs, He gave me peace of mind. I developed a relationship with Him and found solace in my Bible, which I kept close to me, even taking it to bed so I could have something or someone to hold on to. I found my comfort clinging to and reading my Bible. I discovered that God would speak directly to me through His Word.

I believe some women or men have turned to other things besides Jesus for comfort, like drugs, alcohol, and affairs to ease the emotional pain.

When expressing my desire that he help me a little at home after returning home with a newborn baby and having a cesarean section, he wanted to go out with his friends. When I expressed my disapproval, he punched me in the face, causing a gushing of blood out of both nostrils. Unable to control the gushing of blood, he took me to the dispensary after leaving my babies, who were just a year apart, with a friend.

During my third pregnancy, I barely saw my husband at home. I started to have extreme abdominal pain and could not move to get out of bed. I could not contact my husband because I did not know his whereabouts. He had been gone for weeks, so I contacted one of his friends, who came over to aid. He helped me get out of bed and helped me into the car; I didn't know where my other two children were when this occurred. Our friend drove me to the hospital, where I was an emergency admission. I was given oxygen via nasal cannula. The Nurse elevated the foot of the bed on shock blocks as I was in shock. The physician could not contact my husband; he was nowhere to be found. He was not at work, and they needed him to sign for my cesarean section in case of an emergency. It was a matter of life and death, so the physician took responsibility and signed the permission form, which I was told later by the Nurse.

I remember having my vital signs and the baby's vital signs checked as I lay semi-conscious yet hearing what was happening around me. Suddenly, I listened to the nurse call out," The baby's heartbeat has gone bad; I can't count it." Then, I heard the doctor say, "We'll have to go in." That was how I delivered my firstborn son. He is now living in a care home as I was not able to care for him and work to support myself. I lived on the twelfth floor in a condo and feared he may have been in danger. I did not have all the aid available that the victims of abuse have offered to them today. He has adjusted well to his care providers, attends programs offered, and appears quite content with life. I have visitation rights and provide for his added needs; remember his Birthdays and Holidays, and he is happy.

My other three children are living well; thanks be to God. My eldest daughter became a Social Worker employed by the State of Hawaii Adult Mental Health Division, the other daughter worked waitressing and as a Greeter for the tour groups coming off the cruise ships arriving in Hawaii, and my youngest son worked as a Corrections Officer for the State of Hawaii.

The psychological abuse was even worse than the physical abuse, if you can imagine. At least with the abuse, my body would eventually heal. But it is much harder to recover when the mind is under attack. Isolation and abandonment plagued me as I endured violent behavior. Should I even think of disagreeing with or leaving? I watched food and coffee grounds thrown all over the floors and walls in irrational, worse than childish behavior, leaving a mess for me to clean up. He had even allowed the rage to take him so far as to chase me down with a car and pin me between the vehicle and a concrete building and, yes, also being cussed at.

I say these things so you will understand how dark this time of my life was. And yet, I stayed in an abusive, empty, loveless marriage for several reasons. I did not want my children to experience being fatherless. It significantly affected my life, as I couldn't bear to see them suffer through this. I also did not want to break my marriage vows before God. I had committed to love and cherish this man until death do us part.

I would pray for him to change his lifestyle and join me in my Church activities, which he refused to do. God gives us all free will; he did not want to change. God will not force anyone to Him; we must freely wish to accept or decline His offer.

I was trapped, unable to leave.

Another reason I continued to remain was because of the advice I received when I sought spiritual help from the Church:

1. God knows you are not dirt.

2. You must submit to your husband as unto the Lord!

When I received this advice, the only thought that ran through my mind was, "But Jesus would not treat me like that!" I found my husband's actions versus the actions Jesus would have had incomparable. It was a matter of sanity and survival.

It seemed like there was nothing or anyone could save me from this pain. I was in despair and felt utterly abandoned. My only hope was in Jesus and the solace I had discovered in His written Word, my Bible.

CHAPTER 4
SUBMITTING TO CHRIST

In addition to my childhood spiritual experiences, more experiences happened when I submitted totally to Christ, my Savior. I became born again instead of being a religious Christian. The Holy Spirit became real to me and taught me through His Word to disregard religious habits and idol worship and have a genuine relationship with the Living God.

During a time of extreme helplessness and pain in my life, I no longer wanted to live and came close to attempting suicide as an escape from my situation. The mental anguish and pain were more than I could endure, and I couldn't see any other way out! Yet, during my struggle, I knew that a Christian was not to take their own life. God was the giver and taker of life. And I knew I would be hell-bound if I did such a thing.

Exodus 20:13 -Thou shalt not kill.

Matthew 5:21 – Ye have heard that by them of old time, Thou shalt not kill; and whosoever shall kill shall be in danger of the judgment:

That, I'm sure, includes killing of one's self.

It was late one evening, and I was home alone. I walked outside to the back of our home and screamed to God at the top of my lungs. I thought God lived in the sky; somewhere beyond the stars was Heaven, and I wanted Him to hear my cry! I did not know He was closer than a brother and would live inside me!

I shouted, "God take my life! I don't want to live anymore!" I did not realize that my cry was scriptural until the Holy Spirit directed me to read this in my Bible.

"Verily, verily I say unto you, except a corn of wheat fall into the ground and die, it abideth alone: but if it die, it bringeth forth much fruit." John 12:24 (KJV)

It was during this revolutionary period of mental and physical anguish that I was BORN AGAIN! If I had not gone through all the abuse, hurt, and pain that I endured in my life, I believe that I would not have drawn as near or would even know and love the Lord as much as I do today.

I discovered a love (Agape) that is beyond measure, which gives unselfishly and unconditionally to all who seek His face–God's love! Agape is a love that does not take but gives His all for me! I am a survivor through all the pain and trauma; I pray you also come to see that as a positive thing!

As I continued my relationship with Christ, I learned to die in the flesh and to live in the spirit. However, the flesh is sometimes weak, and the struggles are real. I thank God for His gift of repentance and forgiveness!

"Watch and pray, that ye enter not into temptation: the spirit indeed [is] willing, but the flesh [is] weak" Matthew 26:41 (KJV).

Being born again makes us new creatures in Christ Jesus.

Dying to the old life and being born anew. No longer just a child of the flesh (my earthly parents) but being born of spiritual seed God's Seed) Born-again into His kingdom and becoming His child.

"Therefore if any man [be] in Christ, [he is] a new creature: old thing are passed away; behold, all things are become new." 2 Corinthians 5:17 (KVJ).

"And that ye put on the new man, which after God is created in righteousness and true holiness." Ephesians 4:24 (KJV).

"And have put on the new [man], which is renewed in knowledge after the image of him that created him." Colossians 3:10 (KJV).

BAPTISM OF THE HOLY SPIRIT

During times of extreme distress, I would kneel and pray my heart out. One day, as I prayed, I was in so much anguish that I remember breaking out in beads of sweat that would run down and off my body. Then, I recollected Jesus sweating beads of blood during His time of anguish in the garden before His crucifixion. Yet! He was obedient to the Father even unto His death on the cross!

Luke 22:44 And being in an agony He prayed more earnestly: And His sweat was as it were great drops of blood falling down to the ground.

During this period of intense meditation, suddenly, out of nowhere, it had been just a hot summer day without any strong winds on the outside. I felt a sudden wind blow into the room and turned to face my living room window. My living room curtain was no longer hanging to the floor as usual; instead, it was upright in the air, blowing towards me.

That was the minute I received the Baptism of the Holy Spirit!

"And suddenly there came a sound from heaven as of a rushing mighty wind, and it filled all the house where they were sitting." Acts 2:2 (KJV).

Also, during that period, I experienced many spiritual dreams. One of the dreams was of people gathered in a room with cloven tongues like fire over their heads.

"And there appeared unto them cloven tongues like as of fire, and it sat upon each of them." Acts 2:3 (KJV).

IDOLATRY

Something of which I was not at first aware was how I worshipped idols due to my Catholic upbringing. I did this by praying to a statue of Mary, which I had bought. I had created an altar with lit candles surrounding the figure. My teacher taught me to worship Mary in Catholic school. The statue was expensive and had a golden rosary on it.

"Thou shalt have no other gods before me." Exodus 20:3 (KJV).

I was convicted by the Holy Spirit about my idol worship when I came across the above Scripture in my Bible. I knew I was not to give the statue to someone else, even though it was expensive and beautiful. Placing it in a paper sack, I pounded it with a hammer and tossed it in the trash. About Mary, the mother of Jesus, I was to love and respect her as our Lord's mother, but I was not to worship her. My worship was to the only living God.

CHAPTER 5

DREAMS AND CHANGE

I began to have a series of dreams! The Bible has multiple examples of God communicating with His people through dreams. One of the most famous dreams in the Bible is that of Joseph. He had numerous dreams, which he told his family.

"And he said unto them, Hear, I pray you, this dream which I have dreamed:" Genesis 37:6 (KJV).

My dreams were much different. I had a series of scary dreams that helped me to realize I was not right with God. Once, I dreamed of falling through rotten floorboards. On another occasion, I was atop a high building and began falling downward. As I fell, I tried grabbing bars to keep myself from falling, but each one I caught was unanchored, so the fall continued. Then, one time, I dreamed I was in a moving vehicle. The vehicle flew off a cliff and into the ocean around this curve. And the last one I remember was of me locked in a room without any windows or doors.

These dreams could be described as nightmares, but I felt they gave me such powerful insight. They could not simply be dismissed as eating something strange the night before. My life was headed in a disastrous direction, downward. I knew doing my own thing without God would lead me in the direction of being hell-bound. Here, I made a 180-degree turn in my life and began seeking God once more!

As I turned to God, I continued to have dreams. But they were about other things now. I dreamt of standing amid a crowd at a Christian function one night. As I watched, I saw a man who looked like a priest dressed in his garments appear. He walked straight towards me with outstretched arms. He laid His hands on the top of my head (Acts 8:19 Saying, give me also this power, that on whomsoever I lay hands, he may receive the Holy Ghost.) KJV then touched my lips (Hebrews 13:15 By him therefore let us offer the sacrifice of praise to God continually, that is, the fruit of [lips] giving thanks to His name.) KJV then laid both hands over my heart (Ezekiel 36:26 A new heart also will I give you, and a new spirit will I put within you: and I will take away the stony heart out of your flesh, and I will give you an heart of flesh.) KJV. I was not allowed to see His face, but I knew it was the Lord in His priestly role, and my dream ended. It was such a vivid dream!

I continued to look after God, and He had become my all—in—all life support. I clung to Him for strength to continue. I was unable to get enough of Him. My Bible was my constant companion day and night. I read His Word, which would speak to me directly; it comforted me, and I felt a love I had never felt before! It was unconditional! All I had to do was to trust and obey.

BREAKTHROUGH

One morning, just upon opening my eyes while still lying in my bed, I heard a still silent voice. It was silent, yet I heard it with my ears. "Abide in me, and I will abide in you!" I knew I had listened to the Lord speak to me, but it was a strange occurrence. I felt no fear and cherished it, not even sharing it with anyone until now. I wasn't entirely sure what He was trying to tell me then, but as the Lord would have it, He had already prepared a confirmation for me.

MY FIRST CALL TO AFRICA

A series of events led up to my confirmation and call to Africa. I loved a famous singer and song back then, so I called the Christian bookstore, and they placed it on order for me—the title of the album Gentle Moments by Evie. Soon after my experience of hearing the Lord tell me to abide in Him, the lady at the Christian bookstore called to inform me that my purchase had arrived and was ready for pickup.

Excitedly, I drove to pick up my music. I noticed a poster advertising a Full Gospel Businessmen's breakfast when I entered the bookstore. A medical doctor was to speak and testify about how the Holy Spirit worked in his medical practice. Of course, working in the medical field, that poster caught my attention, and I wanted to attend.

I looked at the sales lady, and she was helping another customer. Immediately, she started to reach for my purchase, but I suggested she finish taking care of the other customer, and I would continue to browse.

When I walked over to a nearby book display, I looked down, and right in front of me lay this book titled "ABIDE IN CHRIST" by Andrew Murray. Shocked and excited, I picked up the book and bought it with my album *Gentle Moments*. I got excited when I saw the book with its title. That was precisely what the Lord had said to me. I needed to know how to ABIDE IN CHRIST. The discovery of that book was not accidental; I was learning to hear and obey the Holy Spirit.

Our work schedule had not yet been posted, and I was unsure if I could attend the breakfast meeting. I waited for the work schedule, and sure enough, I had that day off; I was so happy!

I called my sister in Christ and asked if she would attend. She agreed, so I scheduled two reservations.

On the morning of the Full Gospel Business Men's breakfast meeting, I drove to pick up my sister in Christ, who was going with me. The brochure for the event was sitting on the dash right in front, which would later prove significant. Along the way, I noticed a couple waiting for the bus. I strongly wanted to pick them up and offer them a ride. I usually do not pick up strangers, so I drove past them. As I drove past them, I felt a heaviness in my spirit, and the further away I went, the more the heaviness increased.

So, I turned my car around, stopped, and offered them a ride. Both husband and wife hopped in my back seat, and he handed me a business card introducing himself as Reverend Robert Quollet (I'm not sure of the spelling), Medical Missionaries Zambia, Africa. I had no idea that the man I picked up was the Baptist Recruiter to Africa. A picture of a wheelchair was on the card. It immediately struck me that the patients that I worked with were either bedbound or in a wheelchair.

Now, how do you explain this? I'm working in the medical field. The speaker of the event I am about to attend is a medical doctor, and my unexpected passenger is a medical recruiter for Africa!

When I showed him the brochure to the Full Gospel Business Men's Breakfast Meeting promoting the speaker as a medical doctor, the Reverend told me he would attend the Conference Breakfast. He had plans to shop for gifts before returning to Haiti, where I believe he would go after his vacation in Hawaii. He also invited me to join them in missions, and I declined because I still had young children at home. I did not try to contact the Reverend even though he gave me his calling card. The card vanished through the years, probably during one of our moves. Besides, the Holy Spirit had more work to do in my life. I needed more preparation and maturity in spiritual warfare. As a baby Christian, I was unprepared for the work the Holy Spirit had me do when I finally made it to Africa—being on the front line as a Prayer Warrior, taking authority in Jesus' Name against demon-possessed individuals. Some required healing, others deliverance. I also had to be equipped with power from on high. I was using the authority given to me in Jesus' Name, covered with His blood for protection and fully clothed in the armor of God. Every good soldier must undergo basic training before entering the battlefield. I was not yet ready or spiritually mature enough to enter Spiritual Warfare.

I was unaware I would have a second call to West Africa, Benin, during the uprising along the Ivory Coast.

But, once again, the timing was not right; I needed more spiritual equipping in preparation before leaving for an area where they practiced witchcraft and voodoo. I arrived at my friend's house with two passengers, which she did not expect. You should have seen the look on her face. She sat in the front seat with me, and I worried that my passenger had not scheduled a breakfast reservation. The Reverend assured me the Lord would work it out, and God did!

The Reverend decided he would pay for my breakfast, and I wanted to pay for his all the while. Anyway, my breakfast was on him, praise God!

We entered the conference room and were seated in front of the Speaker's podium. It was an incredible experience.

I returned to the Catholic Church, where I made new friends, joined the Catholic Charismatics, and became actively involved in service to the Lord. I was alive again. I was filled with zeal and energy, motivated to walk in the Spirit. I felt and could imagine or compare myself to a horse just raring to go behind a locked gate in the final moment when the obstacle no longer remains—experiencing feelings of release to turn loose and run free.

My call to outreach ministry happened at a Charismatic Service. During break time, I met a sister in Christ and discovered she was a Nurse. We talked and shared for a while, and then I found out she was involved with Catholic Social Services. She invited volunteers to do free physical exams for seniors at the Haleiwa Gym, where lunch was available. Of course, I was so excited I told her I would go.

I waited for the van to pick me up before Long's Drugs Pearl City on the appointed day. I hopped into the ministry van; my first ministry experience awaited me! Upon arrival, my assignment was to do the audiograms in a designated room where I could do the testing. As I waited in the gym, I watched the seniors as they did their activities. Suddenly, as I saw, I was looking at a group of sheep milling around. Then, a little old Japanese woman came waddling towards me, holding an empty paper cup. She asked if I could get her some water and handed me the empty cup. As I reached for it and started towards the water fountain, a thought flashed through my mind. "When you do it unto the least of these, you do it unto Me!" (Matthew 25:40). I once knew I was walking with Jesus!

MY NEW ASSIGNMENT

My Nursing Days

I started working for Beverly Enterprises, a long-term care facility that provides skilled and intermediate care. My new job was as a Medication Nurse. I experienced the Holy Spirit compellingly working through me during my employment there. As I cared for the terminally ill and at the end of life, I could feel the strong presence of the Lord walking with me.

I was newly born again, a baby Christian, filled with the Spirit and freshly empowered with the gifts of the Holy Spirit. I recall a few experiences that occurred during my employment there.

The first experience was a Japanese man who was terminally ill with cancer.

He needed pain meds every four hours and kept a schedule pasted to his bed rail. His wife would visit daily. She sat on a chair beside his bed and quietly saw everything.

One day, he rang for his pain meds, and I responded to his call. His wife was not there, and he was very anxious. I responded to his request and gave him his shot. He grabbed my arm just as I was trying to leave the room. I could tell by the fear in his eyes that I would need to take a moment to pray with him. I began by asking him if he was a Christian.

He said, "Yes."

Then, I asked him if he had ever invited Jesus into his heart.

He said, "No."

Here was a man who claimed to be a Christian, yet he had never accepted Jesus as Savior.

I asked him if I could pray with him. He held tight to my hand as though he did not want me to leave and said, "Yes!"

I prayed, and he accepted the Lord. Then I said, "Now that you have Jesus in your heart, you will not be alone anymore."

He nodded, "Yes," and released his hold on me.

I left the room excitedly, knowing I had just led someone to the Lord.

When I reported for the morning report at the nurses' station the following day, I was surprised that she had not updated me on my new convert. So, I asked about him.

The night shift nurse replied, "Oh! He died last night."

Although initially shocked by her response, I continued my day, peacefully knowing he had gone to be with the Lord in heaven.

I eventually resigned from my position at this facility and moved to another. Nearly a year after this event, I sat across the table from another nurse on our coffee breaks. As we talked for a while, I felt that I had known her from the past. So, I asked her, "Don't I know you from somewhere?"

She responded, "Yes, you took care of my husband before he died, and since then, I have become a born-again Christian." I glanced at her name tag and recognized the name. She was the wife who quietly sat in the room each day as we took care of her husband. The same patient I had the opportunity of leading to the Lord. WOW!

I shared with her that I had prayed with her husband the night he had died, and he had accepted Christ as his Lord and Savior. Her eyes filled with tears; until now, she had no idea where he stood with God. Now, she knew she would one day see him again. I left and have not seen her again.

Another patient came to mind. He was one of fifty-two other residents we had on the floor. He was a Filipino man who had a right leg amputation and was now wearing a prosthesis.

As I prepared to do my morning med round, I pushed my med cart out of the room where we'd stocked it and noticed this man struggling to put on his prosthesis. I expected one of the nursing assistants would help him, so I had my job. As I tried to push my med cart past him as he sat in his wheelchair, he stopped me and asked me to aid him. For some reason, I did not refuse. I locked and parked my cart and started to help him. As I did so, he went ahead to tell me his story. I listened as I fastened his prosthesis.

He had been in a car accident and died. Immediately, an angel came and took him by the hand. The angel escorted him to Heaven. He said the angel went with him through the first door, where he saw a river of crystal-clear water. Then, the angel told him he could not go through the second door because he was not ready. So, he came back, and that was how he lost his leg. His story stunned me as I had just read The Book of

Revelation and remembered reading about crystal clear water in Heaven.

"And he shewed me a pure river of water of life, clear as crystal, proceeding out of the throne of God and of the Lamb." Revelation 22:1 (KJV).

I asked him if he knew that crystal-clear water flowed from the throne, as the Bible says. He said," No."

How could this man describe the river of crystal-clear water unless he had been to Heaven? He was not aware of that passage of scripture!

He must have been there, in Heaven!

I responded, "You have a second chance to make things right with God."

I completed my task and continued with my med round.

On another occasion, a Buddhist woman had a Buddhist Shrine on her nightstand beside her bed.

I had no personal contact with her, but her daughter, who worked in food service at the same facility, was a Born-Again Believer in Jesus Christ. One day, while attending a Christian function, we ran into each other, recognized our kinship in Christ, and became very close friends (or, as we say, sisters in Christ).

She would visit her mother, the woman with the shrine. Her mom was a tiny, older woman curled up in a fetal position lying in bed.

When my sister-in-Christ came on the floor, she would always wave excitedly at me as she could see me preparing meds behind a glass enclosure in the med room. I always waved back at her; she loved the Lord, and our Spirits rejoiced when we saw each other.

She had asked me to agree with her in prayer for her mother to accept the Lord, as she knew her mom's days would soon come to an end. My friend also shared that her mother had refused each time she would talk to her about Jesus. This sister in Christ of mine was very burdened for her mother. I agreed, and we both prayed for her mother's salvation. One day, I heard knocking on the glass window; she was excited with unspeakable joy, waving at me to come out. She wanted to speak with me. I stopped what I was doing and went outside of the med room to talk with her.

She said her mom had told her that Jesus had come to her in a dream. He told her to get rid of the shrine and follow Him! So, the daughter removed the shrine from her mom's room and burned it. We had such a day of rejoicing together. Her mother was now Heaven-bound, and her concern lifted. Hallelujah!

As the days went by, once more, I saw my Japanese Sister in Christ knocking at my med room window, all excited again! Here, I came to discover that Jesus has a sense of humor! LOL, We had a resident in the facility who would propel himself in his wheelchair and wander freely around our floor. His first name was Jesus. Jesus always wore his baseball cap with the name JESUS printed in large letters in front. He never bothered anyone and was always peaceful in his world, but he was confused. One day, in his confusion, he wandered into my friend's mother's room, probably thinking it was his room. He placed his cap with the name JESUS right where the shrine had been sitting and left it there!

My friend giggled as she shared this with me. "Guess what??? Jesus came to visit my mom today and left his cap!" She had walked in to visit her mom and saw the cap with the name JESUS on it in the same spot where the shrine used to be. Well, we both cracked up laughing! YES! Jesus does have a sense of humor. I don't think for one minute that it had been an accident!

I recall noticing one of my male patients wide-eyed, wildly reaching out, trying to grab onto something as he grasped and reached out to an unknown and invisible thing in the empty air around him. His demeanor was one of horror and total fear. All I could think of was my dream of grasping for something to hold on to as I was in a downward direction. I could feel and relate to his experience, so I quietly walked over and touched him. He calmed down at once, and a transformation occurred before my eyes. The Peace of God, which passes all understanding, was transferred from my hand to him at once as I knew the Holy Spirit in me reached out to comfort him. I did not feel led to do anything more; the room was not private, and I had been doing something else at the time.

The last patient I want to tell you about is a white male who had cancer. The room I would deliver meds to had two patients. One of the men was always alert, and the other was semi-comatose. The cancer had metastasized. His right eye protruded out of its socket. As I saw him, I once knew the Lord wanted me to pray with him as I felt a heaviness in my spirit! When this happened, I knew the heaviness would increase if I did not obey the Holy Spirit's prompting. This scenario created a problem for me. I knew I could get into trouble if I got caught praying with someone on company time.

I reasoned with the Holy Spirit I could not do it. I pleaded with Him that I could not pray with that individual because I was bound to use company time appropriately. If I prayed, I would need privacy as the resident in the next bed was quite alert and could report me to my supervisor! As I reasoned with the Holy Spirit, a nurse's aide entered the room, pushing a wheelchair. She approached the resident sitting at his bedside and told him to get into the wheelchair; then, she wheeled him outside the room. That was my first excuse. I was standing there in amazement, and then I watched as the door started to swing shut slowly. There went both my excuses out the window. What caused that door to close shut? Was it the movement of the wheelchair as they passed through, or did an Angel close that door? I'm not sure till today! Thank you, Jesus! I always ask for permission from my residents before praying with them! I prayed with him and left the results in the Lord's hands. He could not respond, but the hearing was one of the last things to go. An individual may be unresponsive but can hear. As for his response, it was just between him and the Lord. I pray he responded affirmatively in his heart.

There was just one refusal to the invitation to Jesus. A woman declined because she said, "My husband was a Buddhist, so I will die a Buddhist." She made her choice. We all have free will to accept Jesus into our lives or decline.

John 3:16 For God so loved the world, that He gave His only begotton Son, that whosoever believeth in Him should not perish, but have eternal life.

CHAPTER 6

MARRIAGE

Years went by; my children were grown and left home. I poured myself out at my job as it gave me purpose and joy. Helping others was always something I wanted to do. I knew what it felt like to be in a helpless position. I realized that doctors were limited in what they could do for people! Jesus was the answer; He is the Great Physician; we are all destined to die someday. The most important thing is eternal life, where an individual would finally end up. I realized the importance of Jesus in our lives; He was the only way to our eternal destination. We make a choice and decide where we will finally end up.

In my previous marriage, I had all the material things: a home, a car, and a beautiful diamond ring studded with added diamonds. Yet, I was miserable and empty. I had all the material things, but I was lonely without the companionship of a husband living his own life.

My relationship with Jesus continued to progress. Jesus was always available to me once I accepted Him as my personal Savior.

Hebrews 13:5b for He hath said, I will never leave thee, nor forsake thee. This scripture leaves me feeling complete. I know I will never again be alone or abandoned.

MY RESCUE FROM ABUSE

One day, out of the blue, one of my cousins from California contacted me. She was still an infant when her parents left Hawaii for California. Now, she was a grown woman, newly graduated from Nursing School, and wanted to know if she could stay with me and vacation in Hawaii for about a week. I agreed, and she came to stay with me and my husband.

After being in our home for a while, one day, she questioned me, "How can you live like this?"

She had noticed my life with my husband when he was at home. I had not said a word to her about my situation of being trapped in my marriage. Or that I felt there was no way out. Then, she invited me to vacation at her home in California. I accepted and was a little surprised to get my husband's permission. But, if I were gone, he would be free to do his own thing without me. It's amazing how God works!

My cousin participated in a Christian Retreat Community for divorced Christians in California. I couldn't have found a more comforting and appropriate place to fellowship. They were actively taking part in services and counseling. I seemed to fit right in. Still, I was battling internally, constantly hitting a wall about a divorce—feelings of being trapped with no solution in sight.

I also found myself involved with home prayer meetings and fasting, in which my cousins participated.

I was in California; my mom was in Hawaii. She had requested prayers for my stepdad, who had a terminal disease and was receiving blood transfusions. The Lord works in mysterious ways, and He works things out in ways unexpectedly. My cousin requested I call my mom to check my stepdad's progress. I got on the phone call, and while it was ringing before she answered, I heard a voice speaking.

"I am the Lord thy God, and I did not mean for you to suffer physical and mental abuse!"

I almost collapsed; I remember wailing uncontrollably, my legs collapsed under me, and my whole body was trembling. My cousin came to my aide, and my mom answered the phone as this was happening. I knew my mom would panic if she heard me wailing, so I stiffened up. The strength of the Lord composed me out of concern for Mom; she had enough stress with my stepdad. I asked her how my stepdad was doing. She gave a good report that he was improving. I ended my telephone call and collapsed once more.

My cousin helped me to a chair as I continued wailing. I finally got my release; it was directly from my Heavenly Father. I felt free to go ahead in obtaining my freedom from bondage.

My cousin questioned me, "Run that by me again?"

I repeated to her what had just occurred.

She said, "Let's pray about this!"

We had been fasting. My two cousins and I walked to the kitchen table, sat, joined hands, and prayed. She prayed out loud, "Lord if this is of you, give us a sign."

Immediately above us, the light directly above the table dimmed until it was ready to go out and brightened three times!

None of us uttered a word after that.

I recognized the light, and the number three had great significance and was my confirmation message. Jesus is the light of the world. There are three persons in the Godhead. Father, Son, Holy Spirit.

John 8::12

Then spake Jesus again unto them saying, I am the light of the world; he that follows me

shall not walk in darkness, but shall have the light of life.

1 John 5:7 KJV "For there are three that bear record in heaven, the Father, the Word, and

the Holy Ghost: and these three are one."

I returned to Hawaii and went ahead with my divorce. I never returned home.

Everything I had, I left behind. I remembered the threat that if I ever left, he would take a contract out on my life. That was the end of my ordeal. Interestingly, the light above the kitchen table did not flicker before or after the response to our prayer request.

I have learned I can trust in God no matter what because I am His child, and He will never leave or forsake me.

"I will not leave you comfortless: I will come to you." John 14:18 (KJV).

"What man of you, having an hundred sheep, if he lose one of them, doth not leave the ninety and nine in the wilderness, and go after that which is lost, until he find it?" Luke 15:4 (KJV)"Peace I leave with you, my peace I give unto you: not as the world giveth, give I unto you. Let not your heart be troubled, neither let it be afraid." John 14:27 (KJV).

I had lost all trust in men and had no intention of ever having another relationship during this period of my life, and I had my freedom. Mom had extended her home to include an extra bedroom, so I moved back home. I was free as a bird, independent, working, and serving the Lord. I bought my Sports car. I had always driven Mustangs, but I bought a Dodge Charger this time because it appealed to me.

LEAVING THE CATHOLIC CHURCH

During this period, I left the Catholic faith because of conflict in my spirit. I wasn't comfortable with some of the teachings because they were not always Scriptural. As I continued to read my Bible, I noticed the discrepancies. I started attending an Assembly of God Church. Here is where the accuracy of the King James Bible replaced previous interpretations in my life.

There, I got very involved in ministry. The pastor was very much into church involvement and outreach. I attended every class and learned about Baptism of the Holy Spirit, Gifts of the Holy Spirit, etc. I was finally receiving solid Scriptural teaching.

I attended all the training sessions and became involved with 700 Club, Women's Aglow, Prison Bible Study, Sunday School, and Stephen's Ministry. I felt invigorated; my life was feeling complete.

MOVING ON WITH LIFE

I also immersed myself in my U.S. Government job at Schofield Barracks, Hawaii. It was a federal position requiring special clearance, as I would have to enter restricted areas where the men worked. My job description involved screening federal employees, conducting health counseling, and giving instructions on properly wearing protective equipment in compliance with OSHA Regulations. I also received training (Audiograms) to check hearing loss before physical exams.

My vehicle had a military decal so that I could drive on base. I lived in the Waianae Coast area, where Mom's home was. I could take the short route to Schofield through the Kolekole Pass, where the Japanese planes had entered Hawaii to attack Pearl Harbor. I enjoyed the special status of entering through the military gate from the Waianae side of Oahu and saw the military guard each morning as he clicked his heels, saluted, and then waved me on. An army guard was stationed at the gate, dressed in full uniform, holding a rifle over his shoulders; beautiful, so patriotic. I was happy, and my life flowed in the right direction, on the straight and narrow path.

CHAPTER 7
THE WOLF IN SHEEP'S CLOTHING

One day, as I attended church, a nice-looking gentleman sat beside me during the service. After several encounters, I was impressed, thinking he would be perfect and we would have much in common. I continued my friendship with him, not knowing who he was. We seemed to be on the same page when I met him in Church.

As time went on, things became serious, and I noticed he was always around where I was.

Some family members who knew him from the past tried to warn me about him. It was a known fact that he was a womanizer who enjoyed living off women, and I just ignored it.

After our marriage, we found a house on the beach with doors that opened right onto the beautiful white sands of Waianae. We had to evacuate our home during that period due to a hurricane. He didn't want to leave to protect our belongings from looters. I drove from our beach house to Mom's in Maile, Hawaii, outside the evacuation zone. Bumper-to-bumper traffic was moving very slowly, the highway along the coastline flooded, and the ocean waves were hitting the sides of my yellow Mustang. My car stalled, causing other drivers to honk at me and, worst of all, to become irate. I sat in my car alone, the waves crashing alongside my car and the drivers going around my stalled car in the middle of the flooded highway. Drivers were yelling at me to move out of the way. Of course, I did not know what to do; I was helpless!

I also did not know that God had already prepared a rescue plan. I made multiple attempts to start the engine; it would only sputter, and then it went completely dead. I looked out my window to see a local man holding a rope alongside my car. He told me he had been at home watching TV, and the Lord told him someone would need help, so he took a rope for towing. Amazingly, he was in a truck right in the back of my car. He hauled my Mustang onto the Cornet Store parking area and drove me to Mom's house. I was able to retrieve my Mustang the following morning! Praise God from Whom all blessings flow.

My husband didn't have a job. I paid the rent and bought all the groceries. I would come home from work and lug all the groceries into the house while he napped with his son. At that time, his son was twelve and had just entered intermediate school. After a while, it began to get on my nerves, and I insisted he find a job. Lo & behold, he found a job as a Service Station Manager. This was good because my insisting he find a job put much pressure on our marriage.

I soon discovered he had his women employees at our home. One day, I was coming home from work, and one was leaving. When I confronted him about this, the excuse was that she came to pick up her paycheck. But she was not the only female employee I had seen at the house. Lots of arguments occurred over this. Then, one day, he left. Around that same time, much money had disappeared from the service station where he worked. My Pastor offered spiritual support; my mom and stepdad were there for me.I continued working and was still very involved with ministry.

OFF TO IDAHO

Me In Idaho With My Dog Mishka

A year went before I heard anything from him. Then, Mom received a phone call from him requesting to speak with me; we were still married. That call was unexpected; I was surprised as he had disappeared into thin air. He called to tell me he had moved to Sandpoint, Idaho and wanted me to join him there. He told me he didn't have a job but would get one. I resigned from my position, made my flight reservations, and left Hawaii on my way to Sandpoint, Idaho.

My mom and stepdad were livid; they strongly recommended that I not go. I decided to try it; I still cared a lot for him. My stepdad threw my suitcases into the trunk of his car. The silence was piercing as he drove me to the airport.

When I arrived in Idaho, it was still spring; everything was beautiful. Fishing for trout, catfish, and bass was so much fun. I loved watching the Mallards as they swam single-file across the pond. It mesmerized me. The beauty of nature was at its best. Of course, I needed someone to bait my hook. I was not going to touch those wiggling worms with my hands.

I had a good-sized savings account, which my husband managed to have me turn over to him to pay the contractor when we were building a house. I'm not sure why I was such a trusting soul or just plain dumb, whichever it was. But I did it.

All seemed to be going well, except it soon became evident he would not make an effort to contribute to the living expenses, and I was finding it difficult to continue caring for two dependents.

We attended an Assembly of God church and visited a Missions Training body of believers. The gifts of the Spirit were in operation; we became family, and they would drop in to see us occasionally.

Winter caught me unprepared. While I did have the proper clothing to keep warm, seeing all white outside caused me to hyperventilate; I felt I couldn't breathe because I was accustomed to Hawaii's greenery! When I saw the thermometer drop thirty below zero, I panicked. I hadn't even realized that was something that could happen! Snow was all around me, and no green trees could be seen.

I strongly wanted to do outreach at the local nursing home during this period. Arrangements were made, and I was granted permission to have Church with the Residents! As I progressed in ministry outreach, I saw less and less of my husband. He was always gone, supposedly looking for work, which he had never found. Tensions were building up within our marriage once again.

THE DARKNESS INSIDE

One day, he took me hunting after borrowing the pastor's rifle. I went with him into the forest to look for a bear. Good gracious, I didn't realize the danger I would have been in should a bear come in our direction. He was equipped with a rifle; I was equipped with Jesus!

Things continued to escalate and become increasingly heated in our relationship. It was winter, our finances were gone, and the pressure was on. I was stressed and contacted my spiritual leaders by phone.

One day, the missionary pastor and his wife unexpectedly visited. I was highly distressed and withdrawn. The pastor's wife approached me and quietly asked if I was being abused. I told her what was happening, and she recommended that I pack a bag and stay overnight at her lovely home in the forest area. She fixed a bed for me to spend the night. I joined them in a home church service they had scheduled for the missions' students. She drove me back home the following day.

My husband was at home waiting for me to return. Our house was in an isolated area of a beautiful forest filled with Tamarack and other large trees.

He was quiet as I sat in the living area. Then I noticed him sitting across from me, holding and messing with the rifle as he faced it in my direction, aiming at it towards me.

Just at that moment, our church elders pulled into our driveway. The pastor had sent them to pick up his rifle. As they entered, I told them what had just occurred. They confronted him verbally, and he denied it. I heard one of the elders say, "Don't tell me you were not facing the rifle at her!"

The elder believed what I had told him. The elders retrieved the rifle and returned it to the pastor.

A few days later, the Missionary Pastor came to the house accompanied by a couple of other elders of the Church. They had come to pray for my husband.

I listened and watched them lay hands on him and prayed. I heard the Pastor ask him about his behavior. I discovered he had been carrying a bear claw and a small medicine bag. His grandfather was a Native American traditional healer who taught him the arts. Then, out of his mouth, a strange voice said, "It's because souls will be saved!" An eerie laugh followed this. Whatever spirit was in him became more agitated when I decided to return to ministry.

The Pastor stopped praying that day and later told me he could not complete the deliverance because my husband was not ready. He explained that it was like a boil that could not be lanced because it wasn't ripe yet.

2 Corinthians 6:14 Be ye not unequally yoked together with unbelievers: for what fellowship hath righteousness with unrighteousness? And what communion hath light with darkness?

The Bible warns about being unequally yolked in marriage. Not having the same spirit or beliefs affects one's marriage, bringing division and strife. I realize today that this was a significant problem in my previous marriages. I was vigorously practicing my faith, which irritated their spirits or may have been the cause of most of the issues I encountered. Others may claim to believe in faith in Jesus but not fully submit to Christ, having a different spirit.

A Christian should be filled with the Holy Spirit, or other spirits come in to inhabit the individual.

Ephesians 5:8 And be not drunk with wine, wherein is excess; but be filled with the Spirit;

Matthew 12:45 Then goeth he, and taketh with him seven other spirits more wicked than himself, and they enter in and dwell there: and the last state of that man is worse than the first.

ALONE ONCE MORE

After that occurrence, he abandoned me. I was left alone at home in the middle of winter with no heat. As a woman from Hawaii, I did not know how to protect myself against the elements.

Thankfully, both Pastors checked my situation by telephone and gave me the support I needed. My Assembly of God Pastor, with his wife, plugged a small heater into the wall outlet. I watched them grab sheets and towels to pad the floor baseboards to keep the cold air out. There was a furnace downstairs, but I had no wood, and even if I did have wood, I would not have known how to set it up.

Pastor's wife drove to my aid. My car had slid on black ice, causing it to slide into a shallow ditch alongside the road. I did not know about chains on tires. She brought chains with her, and I can still see Pastor's wife lying on the icy road, putting chains on my tires. She was wearing her blue jeans. I didn't know about black ice until I found my car sliding uncontrollably on the road and ending up in a ditch. I learned the hard way. Thank you, Jesus, for all the help you sent me.

Starving, cold, and without money to buy food, I entered a small restaurant and sat, dazed, not knowing what to do. The server asked if I wanted to order something. I said, "No," since I didn't have money to pay for food. As I sat alone towards the back of a booth, the owner approached me, put his hand on my shoulder, and offered me a free meal. Also, he told me if I was ever hungry again, I could return. WOW! Isn't that just like something God would do? As I left, I noticed a poster on the front door. The information was a phone number to the Prosecuting Attorney's Office for abused women. Apparently, at the time, it was a big problem in the area.

My only hope was to call Mom in Hawaii. They had warned me, but I didn't listen. My mom was very understanding; she sent me a plane ticket and some money. In their kindness, the pastor and his wife let me use their daughter's room and placed her with her little brother in his room, providing a much-needed sense of relief and comfort.

My pastor, in a rare act of justice, told me he had only given two people permission for a divorce. The first was a lady whose husband had been sexually abusing his daughter, and the second person was me. Pastor contacted his friend, a Christian Attorney who was busy organizing a crusade. He agreed to take my case. I told him I didn't have any money. He responded, "I have never seen any Christian who did not pay their bills." He said I could pay him later. We went to court, and my husband was a no-show. My divorce was granted, a moment that filled me with empowerment and freedom. I sold my car and paid my attorney. My pastor and his wife drove me to the airport in the church van, and I was returning home to Hawaii. I was handed a sealed envelope, which my Sandpoint pastor had written to my Hawaii pastor. I never was told what the letter contained.

DIVORCED BUT NOT FORGOTTEN

Christian marriages can sometimes place a person in bondage because some self-righteous Christians strongly recommend against divorce. A person is made to feel inferior even though divorce is a sin like any other, and it can be forgiven. Now, I'm not trying to justify divorce, but sometimes it is the only alternative. Divorce is not an unpardonable sin. Besides, I like to stand on this Scripture, "For whosoever shall keep the whole law, and yet offend in one [point], he is guilty of all." James 2:10 (KJV).

So, when you commit one sin, you commit all! That causes me to understand that everyone who commits one sin is also guilty of the sin of divorce. God does not differentiate one sin from another; all sin separates us from God. That is why Jesus died. We are all sinners and fall short of the glory of God. God is holy and cannot look upon sin. He could not look upon His own Son when he bore the sins of the whole world on the cross. Jesus paid the price for all sin, including the sin of divorce. Some have just been unfortunate to have been caught in the snare of divorce.

The stigma of being a divorcée can cause a person to be discriminated against and feel inferior. Not all marriages are made in Heaven. Being unequally yoked, a term used in the Bible to describe a relationship where one partner is not a believer, is a big problem, especially when others refuse to submit to God's authority. Yes, some may convert and come to the Lord eventually, but the other person's life can be in danger if they refuse. There have been husbands who kill their wives and vice versa. Those who are fortunate to have good marriages are indeed blessed.

My opinion on the divorced person is that Jesus, in all of His mercy and compassion, would say, "Go and sin no more." And to the self-righteous person who wanted to condemn them for getting a divorce, "Who will throw the first stone?" Spousal abuse stems from man's fallen nature. It took God's unconditional love (Jesus) to free the captive. The problem is that love has been marred and distorted by sinful men. Instead of having the pure love of God (Agape), the enemy of our souls offers a counterfeit called lust—man's sinful nature. "For the flesh lusteth against the Spirit, and the Spirit against the flesh: and these are contrary the one to the other: so that ye cannot do the things that ye would." Galatians 5:17

SIN & FORGIVENESS

God created people in His image. God is Love. He started the first marriage with Adam and Eve in the Garden of Eden. Still, sin has dramatically distorted God's image and the perfect union of man and woman from God's plan to what it has now become."So God created man in his [own] image, in the image of God created he him; male and female created he them." Genesis 1:27 (KJV).

"He that loveth not knoweth not God; for God is love." 1 John 4:8 (KJV).

God had a plan, and Satan did, too. By disobeying God's command, Eve, the weaker vessel, became a target. She fell and tempted Adam, her husband, opening the door to sin and a curse that went from generation to generation. The serpent beguiled Eve, who in turn seduced Adam.

It records a woman's strong influence over a man. Adam loved Eve so much that he was willing to disobey God.

"And when the woman saw that the tree was good for food and that it was pleasant to the eyes, and a tree to be desired to make one wise, she took of the fruit thereof, and did eat, and gave also unto her husband with her, and he did eat." Genesis 3:6 (KJV).

In his fallen nature, man can only be redeemed today by the sacrificed Lamb of God, His only begotten Son, Jesus. By the shed blood of Jesus on the cross, our Heavenly Father God offered a way of escape to those who will accept His gift of love, mercy, and forgiveness.

Our Heavenly Father knows our weaknesses and frailties. He also provided the Holy Spirit to comfort, teach, and empower His pitiful creatures vulnerable to temptation. I do not understand how people can go through life without God.

We live in a Godless society where man has declared himself to be a god instead of being empowered by the Holy Spirit of God.

Satan hates God after he was cast out of Heaven with one-third of the angels. Lucifer wanted to overthrow God and become a god. He was also full of pride, being the most beautiful of the angels; music flowed from his body.

Being cast down from Heaven, he became the god of this world. Father God's ultimate sacrifice restores man to God. We all have a choice to make. We can become a child of God or continue to fall under the dominion of the fallen one. The question remains: who is your father? We must choose God as our father and accept His Son Jesus as our redeemer to be a child of God, to enter His Kingdom.

"Verily I say unto you, Whosoever shall not receive the kingdom of God as a little child shall in no wise enter therein." Luke 18:17 (KJV).

"In this, the children of God are manifest, and the children of the devil: whosoever doeth not righteousness is not of God, neither he that loveth not his brother." 1 John 3:10 (KJV).

God's Word prepares, equips, and warns His children. The problem is that most people may not study their Bibles or may have difficulty understanding the written Word.

There was a time when I read and did not understand, but after receiving the Holy Spirit, I understood the written Word more clearly. It became alive and straightforward, almost like I had my tutor. The Holy Spirit illuminated the Word to my understanding.

"But the Comforter, [which is] the Holy Ghost, whom the Father will send in my name, shall teach you all things, and bring all things to your remembrance, whatsoever I have said unto you." John 14:26 (KJV).

AVAILABLE RESOURCES

If, by chance, you are reading this book and are also in an abusive relationship, I would advise you to contact your spiritual advisor, who should be able to help you and offer referrals to agencies that can provide you with the help you need. Multiple resources are available to abused people today, which were not available at the time of my troubles. I encourage you to get the help you need so you can experience freedom from the bondage that you have been suffering through.

National Domestic Violence Hotline

Hours: 24/7

Call 800 -799-7233

Text BEGIN to 88788

CHAPTER 8

MY RESTORATION

Back home in beautiful Waianae, Hawaii, I was once more secure with blood relatives and my spiritual family who loved, cared for, and protected me. My pastor was very supportive, always caring for his little flock. It was a healing experience to be loved and supported by caring individuals who accepted me back into the fold without judgment or accusations. I was working once more alongside and enjoying my physical and spiritual family's fellowship.

I was home where it was warm and green, with fragrant flowers, plain country folk, the beautiful blue ocean, glistening white sandy beaches, and waves hitting the seashore—peaceful, laid-back living—running barefoot in the sand once more. Without a care in the world, I regained my life, healed, and restored. Again, I poured myself out, helping those going through their pain and struggles as a Stephen's Minister and telephone responder with the 700 Club, Bible Studies at the prison, and nurse to the lonely and abandoned elderly. There are so many wounded walking around, just trying to hold themselves together. Emotional pain is as correct as a physical wound, sometimes even worse since a band-aid does not do the trick.

My new job was in Waianae, Hawaii, just a short drive from Mom's home to Leeward Nursing Home, where I worked the evening shift. I was responsible for fifty residents, meds, treatment, doctor's orders, supervision of nurses' aides, and legal documentation of residents' daily progress, care, interventions, etc. I loved my residents as family and ensured they were cared for with dignity. I knew the Lord had entrusted their care to me and would be accountable if I neglected my responsibilities.

MY DILEMMA WITH BUDDHA

One of my nurses' aides approached me and asked if I would like to contribute money towards buying a Buddhist statue as a gift to the facility's owner for her birthday. She said all those who contributed would have their name engraved on the plaque. As a follower of Christ, I knew I couldn't and wouldn't do that, even if it was for my boss. The thought and reply that I gave her, "No! I don't need to have my name printed on the plaque; my name is already written in the Book of Life!"

Revelation 3:5 He that overcometh, the same shall be clothed in white raiment; and I will not blot out his name out of the book of life, but I will confess his name before my Father, and before His angels.

.

I felt uncomfortable attending the function and was hesitant to participate due to a conflict in my spirit over this Scripture:

"For if any man see thee which hast knowledge sit at meat in the idol's temple, shall not the conscience of him which is weak be emboldened to eat those things which are offered to idols;" 1 Corinthians 8:10 (KJV).

In my dilemma, I consulted with my pastor, who told me it would be okay to attend and partake of the food. As I entered my boss's home, a massive statue of Buddha sat in the front room, facing the front door. I also noticed the food and fruit placed in front of the figure. I felt very uncomfortable as I passed in front of it, and I did not know then that God would turn it around for good. As we entered a single file for our food, our boss unexpectedly asked me to pray and bless the food before partaking. I said a prayer out loud for all to hear and ended it in Jesus' name. Then everyone ate their food. My discomfort was gone, and I rejoiced internally, knowing Jesus had honored me and, in turn, I had honored Him. Praise God from whom all blessings flow.

DEATH AND MISUNDERSTANDING

My stepdad had passed on due to his terminal disease. Mom was distraught, so I took family emergency leave from work. I took a leave of absence for a couple of weeks. When I returned to work, I overheard a conversation between a couple of my nursing assistants. I heard, "Should we tell her?" My curiosity was becoming aroused. I looked at the Nursing Assistantshem questioningly and listened to their story.

One of our residents, a tiny, hunched-over Japanese woman with a severe case of arthritis, her hands and fingers badly snarled due to her deformity, was unable to feed herself. During mealtime, I had made it a habit to feed her. In my absence, she became despondent, refusing to eat any food. Someone had approached her during this time and asked her why she wouldn't eat.

She started to cry and said, "My nurse died." She had overheard a discussion about me being gone because my stepdad had passed and misunderstood that I had died. Then they explained to her that it was my stepdad and not me who had died. I felt so sorry for that poor little lady. I hugged her; she was happily eating once more with aid. It seemed easy to bond with the abandoned and suffering since I knew what it was like and could certainly relate to it.

CHAPTER 9

A NEW LOVE

My Husband Bill and I during

"March for Jesus" Hilo, Hawaii

As the years rolled by, my feelings toward men began to change. I started to feel lonely once more. I did not enjoy not having someone with whom I could share my life. Another nurse that I worked with shared the same feeling of loneliness. Of course, we started to go out together as friends. One day, she came up with an idea. We were both Christians, so she suggested I pray for her so the Lord would send her a husband and that she, in turn, pray for me. She said that way, it wouldn't be selfish when we prayed. LOL! It worked, and we soon both got married.

God did not create a person to be alone! There is a deep longing within us that draws us to seek companionship. Not everyone can handle the loneliness of being single. "And the LORD God said, [It is] not good that the man should be alone; I will make him a help meet for him." Genesis 2:18 (KJV).

My husband, a civil engineer, worked and traveled worldwide in foreign countries. He moved to Hawaii and said God told him to come to Hawaii. I was still working the evening shift in the nursing home, and he was working for a construction company in Oahu, Hawaii.

We met at the Makaha Surf Side, where I had bought a condo on the third floor on the beach. My now husband, Bill, had been renting a condo in the same building. We dated; he was a Christian, and we have been married for over thirty-seven years. I continued my church activities, and he joined me at church. We were equally yoked and had the same values and beliefs.

Life goes on; it is not always easy, but it becomes an exciting journey with God. Nothing is impossible with God. He restored me and is still not finished with me.

One day, Bill came home and told me we would be moving to the Big Island of Hawaii. I sold my Condo, resigned from my job, and we moved on.

LIFE ON THE BIG ISLAND

Our move to the Big Island, Hawaii, was quite a learning experience for me.

We rented a house in Mountain View, Hawaii. It had electricity, but the water supply was from the water catchment. A wooden tank sat elevated alongside the house. Rainwater ran off the roof and into the water tank for home use. I wasn't familiar with water catchment and didn't give it much thought. Water flowed from the faucets like it did on Oahu.

I used it for my dishwasher, baths, washing machine, and other things, usually using water without any problems. Then, one day, there was no water for our use. The small wooden water tank ran dry. We had a dry spell and had no rain. So, we took empty containers to the county water spigots, filled them, and took them home. That was a shock for me.

We attended the Kurtistown Assembly of God. I had a letter of recommendation from my pastor at Paradise Chapel to inform my new pastor of my earlier training and church service; by this time, I had been ordained as Stephen's minister and equipped with the gifts of the Holy Spirit. The letter was a good report, so I was available for church ministry, Sunday school teacher, and superintendent. I was also honored to be one of the guest speakers at the Sunday school training of Sunday school teachers in West Hawaii. After the conference, I was shocked when my pastor presented me with an honorarium from the conference organizer. I was usually the giver and not the receiver. I donated it to our Sunday school.

The Department of Water Supply hired my husband, Bill, as a civil engineer, and I worked as a unit coordinator at the Life Care Center in Hilo. I had my evening shift and my floor. With my experience and excellent recommendations from my earlier jobs on Oahu, I had no problem.

We decided to buy three three-acre parcels of land in Hawaiian Acres, close to our church. Everything seemed to be falling into place. We planned on building our home there and wanted to do some farming. One of the church elders took us under his wing as we were unfamiliar with doing things on this Island. Recommendations by the elder helped tremendously. He suggested we put our furniture in storage sheds and live in a trailer while building our home. We did as he told us. We rented a silver bullet-type trailer home. We also completed the driveway, house pad, and cesspool. All was going well until the rains came.

The realtor had advertised the property we had bought as having a seasonal stream. I thought that was wonderful as I envisioned a lovely stream flowing through the property. The stream bed was dry till the rains steadily flooded the area with water waist-high. We discovered that our seasonal stream was a waterway for the past sugarcane plantations. Our newly dug cesspool was overflowing, and our trailer home was close to floating downstream. Thankfully, our friend spared our furnitire as he had suggested we place the storage building on a high hillside on the property. But all this ended that dream.

We moved into another rental until we bought a 1/4-acre uncleared parcel in Hawaiian Beaches. The property was reasonably priced, and we had some experience hiring D9 operators, cesspool diggers, and contractors, so we ventured into our new project. Finally, someone took charge and built our home. moved into it and continued to work at our jobs.

The Pahoa Assembly of God became our new Christian Family. I taught Sunday school and became one of the Youth Leaders. Then, I met a sister in the Lord who lived across the street from our home. She invited me to some home churches in the local Hawaiian communities where special guests and Spirit-filled guest speakers would be brought in to minister and preach. I enjoyed the local home church fellowships; the preaching was Biblical, and the gifts of the Holy Spirit were in operation. We were all "Ohana" (family).

CHAPTER 10
SECOND CALL TO AFRICA

I heard that there would be a Nigerian evangelist speaking at one of the home churches. This particular home church was located in the basement, extending from the garage to the back area amid green grass and giant trees in the Hawaiian homestead of Keaukaha. The congregation was large, and the Hawaiian worship team was entertaining and anointed.

I enjoyed the loving fellowship and the worship team. Upon hearing of the Nigerian guest evangelist, I felt a deep desire to attend, especially since I remembered my past encounter with the Baptist Medical Missionary Recruiter to Africa and his extended invitation years before. In my spirit, I knew I had a calling to go to Africa.

On the evening of the event, I drove along the beautiful coast of Keaukaha and into the Hawaiian Home area where the home church was. The worship was refreshing, with total freedom to worship in the Spirit. The service was structured, but there was also freedom for the Holy Spirit to move unhindered.

Later, I heard that the Nigerian evangelist would speak at an Assembly of God Church in Kona (West Hawaii), and I lived on the Big Island's Hilo side (East Hawaii). I strongly wanted to attend that service, especially since the Kona pastor was an old friend and brother in the Lord. He and his wife attended the same Assembly of God Church in Pacific Palisades that I attended in Pearl City, Hawaii, on the island of Oahu. We had run into each other at McDonald's on the Hilo side, and he had invited me to visit the Assembly of God Church in Kona.

I had already received an invitation from the church pastor to visit their church, and now the Nigerian evangelist was to speak at that same Church.

On the Sunday of the service, my husband, Bill, accompanied me. Together, we drove from East Hawaii to West Hawaii. I decided to kill two birds with one stone, accept the earlier invitation, and listen to the

Nigerian evangelist speak. When we arrived at the church, we were greeted in the parking lot and ushered into the church to our seats. As we waited, the Nigerian evangelist, accompanied by another home church pastor, a friend, and a brother in Christ. I watched the usher escort them to their designated seats directly before us. I sat quietly, not saying a word, then the Nigerian evangelist who sat straight in front of me turned around to face me and, with a massive smile, told me, "Rose, you may be part of the team."

He was selecting a team to do a Crusade in Benin, West Africa. I was totally in shock yet extremely excited within my spirit. That is how the Holy Spirit arranged my second call to Africa. I didn't do it; I obeyed the call and was fully equipped spiritually and prepared.

FROM BELGIUM TO BENIN

A Christian family hosted us in Brussels, Belgium, on our way to Benin. Benin is a French-speaking nation in West Africa and the birthplace of the vodun (more widely known as "voodoo") religion.

We gathered our funds for our trip, obtained the required immunizations to enter the area, made our flight reservations, and obtained the needed passports. Prayer covered the team as we would be entering a place of witchcraft and voodoo.

The pastors of the churches in Benin were in preparation. In the evening, the pastors of the Christian churches organized and held the crusade in an outdoor sports field. It was just a large, empty, sandy area with a stage for speakers, microphones, and lighting surrounding it. Chairs were on the field for guests while the crowds gathered and stood to listen to the speakers.

We rented rooms at a small hotel. Buckets filled with water and a dipper were placed alongside the bathtub for our baths. Bottled water was provided for drinking purposes. Food consisted of fish or steak. The steaks seemed small, and little did I know they were goat meat. I stuck with fish, fries, and salad. Outside of the hotel stood bamboo grass huts alongside the beach. The more prosperous people had brick houses. They made bricks out of sand and mud and then dried them in the sun.

We attended seminars by guest speakers and local pastors. The teachings were Biblical, right out of the King James Bible; the Word was rightly divided. The worship was out of this world; the Church members invited us to take part as we danced to the drums,

I was selected to be on the prayer team. Every night, altar calls were available for those who wanted prayers for healing, deliverance, or whatever they requested.

Since communication was a problem, the crowds were instructed to point to the area needing prayer for healing.

On the first night of the crusade, I saw people standing as far as my eyes could see. The multitude of people were hungry for Jesus to heal them. It was an honor to be on that team. On the first night, when the announcement was made for prayer, we were surrounded by the crowds. The Christian church leaders of all the local churches were concerned as we were buried by the swarms of unsaved seekers wanting to be prayed over. We were required to wear the local attire, which included a head covering.

I recall being surrounded, pushed and shoved as the unsaved wanted to be prayed over by the laying on of hands. As the crowd pressed in, I continued laying hands and praying for as many as possible while surrounded and buried by the masses. I could feel the crowd pressing in.Somehow, my head covering got knocked off my head and onto the ground. I continued praying, trying to touch and reach as many as possible. I felt the anointing of the Holy Spirit, who used me as His vessel. He touched through me. I was just His instrument. Amid the frenzy, suddenly, I felt a touch oh so gentle, tying my headscarf back on my head. I did not see the person as I continued laying hands and praying. At one point, the announcer would tell everyone to shut their eyes while a closing prayer was made over the microphone. That was the signal for the prayer team to escape the crowds.

The local churches joined hands on the second night, forming a circle around the prayer team, keeping the masses from pressing in. Some witches, demon-possessed individuals, and others would go into a spin and fall to the ground, lying flat on their backs as if unconscious on the sandy soil. Then, when they got off the ground after they regained consciousness, they'd give their testimonies of salvation, healing, and deliverance! All we needed to do was raise our hands towards them in prayer without getting close or touching them. It seemed electrifying as the power of God flowed from the prayer warriors to the people. Some on the following nights brought in their healing testimonies from their doctors.

I heard some declare and gesture that they had snakes in their stomachs.

One evening, as I prayed with an individual, the spirits in them would cause them to resist by forcing them to spin and fall under the power of the Holy Ghost. As I prayed with a specific individual, I noticed a scorpion coming straight for me with its tail moving swiftly in the sand. Since I was in intense prayer, I just kicked it out of the way with my covered shoe.

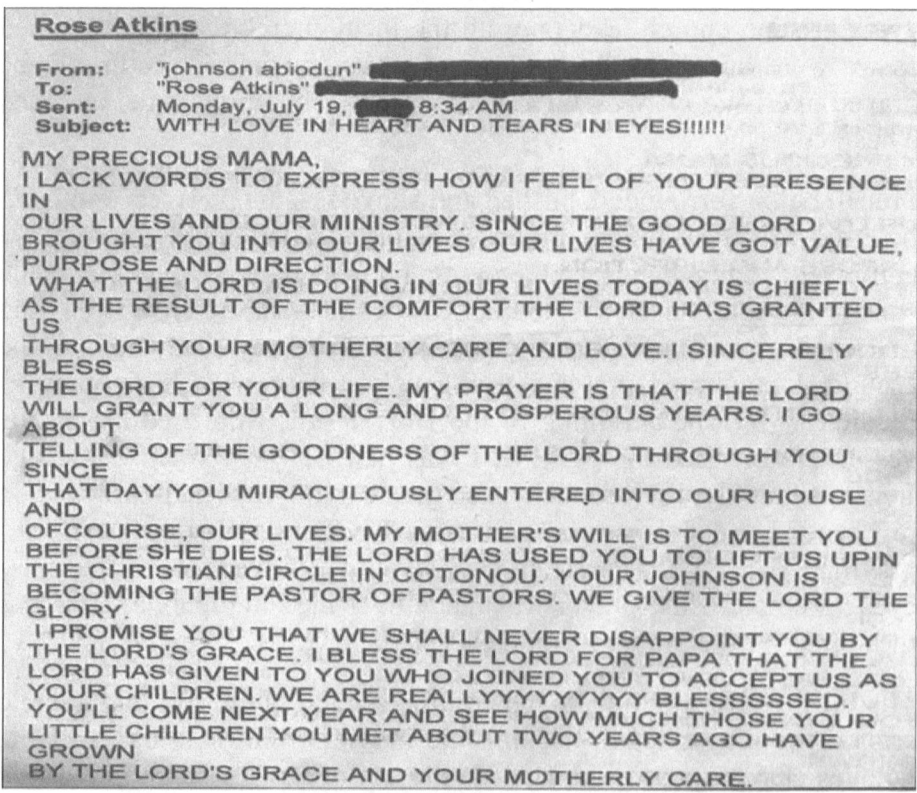

Rose Atkins

From: "johnson abiodun" ▓▓▓▓▓▓▓▓▓
To: "Rose Atkins" ▓▓▓▓▓▓▓▓▓
Sent: Monday, July 19, ▓▓ 8:34 AM
Subject: WITH LOVE IN HEART AND TEARS IN EYES!!!!!!

MY PRECIOUS MAMA,
I LACK WORDS TO EXPRESS HOW I FEEL OF YOUR PRESENCE IN
OUR LIVES AND OUR MINISTRY. SINCE THE GOOD LORD BROUGHT YOU INTO OUR LIVES OUR LIVES HAVE GOT VALUE, PURPOSE AND DIRECTION.
WHAT THE LORD IS DOING IN OUR LIVES TODAY IS CHIEFLY AS THE RESULT OF THE COMFORT THE LORD HAS GRANTED US
THROUGH YOUR MOTHERLY CARE AND LOVE.I SINCERELY BLESS
THE LORD FOR YOUR LIFE. MY PRAYER IS THAT THE LORD WILL GRANT YOU A LONG AND PROSPEROUS YEARS. I GO ABOUT
TELLING OF THE GOODNESS OF THE LORD THROUGH YOU SINCE
THAT DAY YOU MIRACULOUSLY ENTERED INTO OUR HOUSE AND
OFCOURSE, OUR LIVES. MY MOTHER'S WILL IS TO MEET YOU BEFORE SHE DIES. THE LORD HAS USED YOU TO LIFT US UPIN THE CHRISTIAN CIRCLE IN COTONOU. YOUR JOHNSON IS BECOMING THE PASTOR OF PASTORS. WE GIVE THE LORD THE GLORY.
I PROMISE YOU THAT WE SHALL NEVER DISAPPOINT YOU BY THE LORD'S GRACE. I BLESS THE LORD FOR PAPA THAT THE LORD HAS GIVEN TO YOU WHO JOINED YOU TO ACCEPT US AS YOUR CHILDREN. WE ARE REALLYYYYYYYYY BLESSSSSED. YOU'LL COME NEXT YEAR AND SEE HOW MUCH THOSE YOUR LITTLE CHILDREN YOU MET ABOUT TWO YEARS AGO HAVE GROWN
BY THE LORD'S GRACE AND YOUR MOTHERLY CARE.

Letter I received from Pastor Abiodun Johnson after

Returning to Hawaii

The team members were assigned to preach Sunday services to different churches in the area.

Here are a few photos sent to me from Pastor Mark after returning home to Hawaii.

Here I am in the center with Pastor Mark left And my interpreter right of the picture.

Dancing to the Drum Worship during setting up of the Offering Box. Apparently things besides money are brought to the church.

Pastor Mark left with church elders and me.

I was asked to pray with Members in need of Prayer by Pastor Mark

Women and children in front of Church.

Here I am, little ole' me dressed in my African attire, escorted into an automobile with a placard "Pastor" on the dash in front of the windshield. I sat alone in the backseat while two African pastors sat in front and drove me to the church in the outskirts, deep in the village. It seemed like a long drive as we moved away from the populated area. When we arrived, one of the pastors opened the door to let me out. Immediately, I saw a young child running towards me. This child grabbed my Bible and handed me a bottle of water. I had an escort who carried my Bible for me into the hut, which was the church. After the service, a meal was served, with more fellowship, then more dancing to the beat of drums before the arrival of my escorts back to our destination. The people were so warm, accommodating, and loving.

Before we entered a church or building, they held us back until they prayed over our chairs. We were informed it was for our protection, as the witches would conduct spells and curses on where we were to sit before our arrival.

TRIP INTO THE VILLAGE

My team partner was a sister from Uganda. We obtained permission from our superiors to go into the village. We traveled on foot along the hot sand in twos. The villagers recognized us, and some stopped to talk. One woman holding a baby asked if I would pray for her child, who had a burning fever for a few days. The baby, just months old, lay lifeless in his mother's arms. I laid my hand on the child and prayed. As I withdrew, I saw the baby's face light up, glowing brightly as the sun, and he had a massive smile.

Jesus uses simple, everyday people who allow His power to flow through them. I'm not some great evangelist, just a willing vessel ready for the Master's use. I give Him all the glory. As we continued along the way, we came across a man sitting in the shade; he appeared to be busy at work. We chatted, and he invited us to meet his pastor. We agreed, so he walked us to his pastor's house! When I met my spiritual family, whom the Lord had designated, I supported them in their ministry after leaving Africa and returning home.

I shall share pictures and written communications that I have accumulated of our crusade and the crusade harvest of souls by this fantastic family chosen by God.

I shared photos of the village church where I went to preach! After returning to Hawaii, the pastor sent me the pictures via mail. These are fantastic memories—one of the greatest moments of my life.

Indeed, My Heavenly Father can transform darkness into light. My life has been radically transformed. I love my Abba for all He has done to provide, protect, and save me from the fires of hell. My name is written in the Book of Life. I am a child of God!

BORN-AGAIN WOMEN PASTORS

"Therefore if any man [be] in Christ, [he is] a new creature: old things are passed away; behold, all things are become new." 2 Corinthians 5:17 (KJV).

Paul's admonition applies to women who are not born again!

God does use women.

"But ye [are] a chosen generation, a royal priesthood, an holy nation, a peculiar people; that ye should shew forth the praises of him who hath called you out of darkness into his marvelous light;" 1 Peter 2:9 (KJV)

When a person is born again, they are considered new creatures in Christ Jesus, and one in Christ Jesus is no longer male or female in the eyes of God. If God does not discriminate against born-again women or men, then why should we?

"There is neither Jew nor Greek, there is neither bond nor free, there is neither male nor female: for ye all one in Christ Jesus." Galatians 3:28 (KJV)

RESULTS POST CRUSADE BENIN, WEST AFRICA

The Benin Crusade was very rewarding and fruitful!

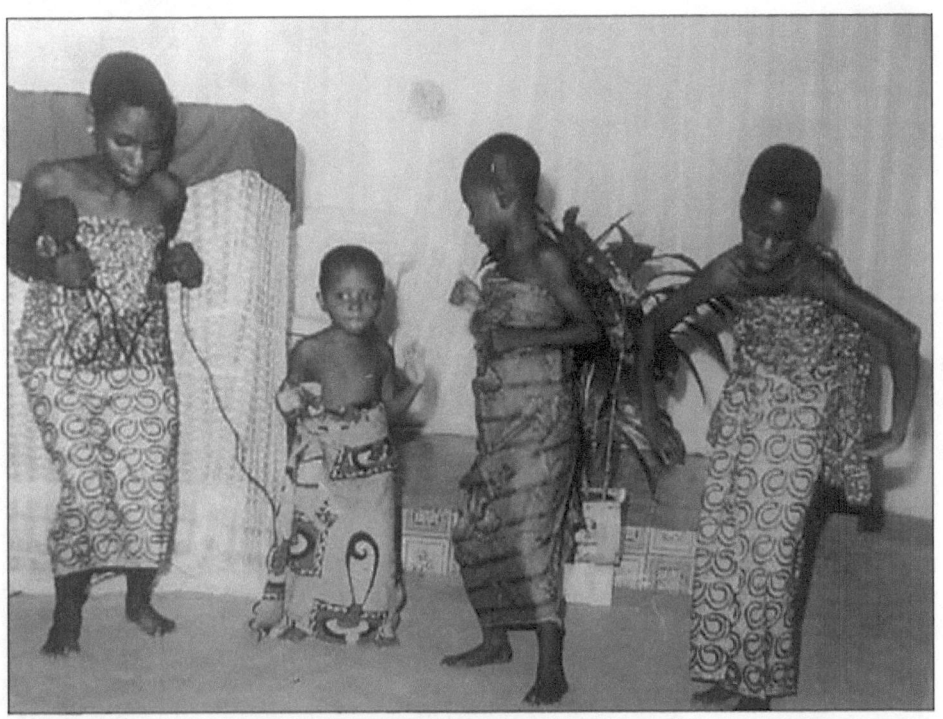

Children worshipping the Lord dancing to drum instruments in Children's Church

Pastor's wife, Pastor Elise, is leading the Children's Church.

Top photo Beach outreach, salvation new souls, and Bible distribution.

Bottom photo new converts with their Bibles.

Living Fountain Ministries International

The souls and the Bibles here

Church at the beach during outreach to unsaved

More beach pictures

Unsaved listening to the Gospel

Hectic traffic in Benin

CHAPTER 11
VOLCANIC ERUPTION

In 2018, while downstairs doing laundry in my carport, I suddenly heard strange noises in the sky above me. As I listened carefully, it sounded like a trumpet blowing. I continued to do my laundry, ignored it, and kept it to myself. I wasn't quite sure what might be happening.

"In what place [therefore] ye hear the sound of the trumpet, resort ye

The people. Done in times of war (see Judges 3:27; 6:34; Nehemiah 4:18–20) as well as at times of celebration, such as a feast or the anointing of a king (see Leviticus 25:9; 1 Kings 1:34; 2 Kings 9:13; Psalm 81:3). Many people heard this trumpet sound in our area that day. They even have some recordings on the internet. Some thought it might be the second coming of Christ, as spoken about in the Bible. It was such an eerie thing, but I genuinely believe the trumpet sounds I heard were warnings from God. Within a few days, a volcanic eruption occurred in our subdivision!

It was a horrible experience, but God turned it all around for good.

Others heard the Trumpet sound! See YouTube Videos:

1. Rapture-like trumpet sounds in the skies above Hawaii. UFO? End times? Live Recording.

2. Trumpet sounds heard in Hawaii. Jeremiah 11:11 2nd Exodus

3. Trumpet sounds 30 days before the volcanic eruption in Hawaii.

4. Trumpet Like Sounds Recorded Over Hawaii

Sirens wailed loudly; Civil Defense ordered an evacuation of the area. I grabbed my purse and car keys, put on my slippers, and hopped into my car to leave the area. Driving on Leilani Avenue, the cars were backed up bumper to bumper as I went to leave the area. Police cars, fire trucks, Civil Defense, ambulances, and the National Guard were at the entrance and exit within our subdivision. Blue lights flashed from emergency vehicles, sirens wailed, and roadblocks surrounded me as I slowly drove out of the area.

The ground in our subdivision had opened, and lava was starting to pop up from the fissures, some of which were on roadways within our subdivision.

Evacuation centers were available to the residents.

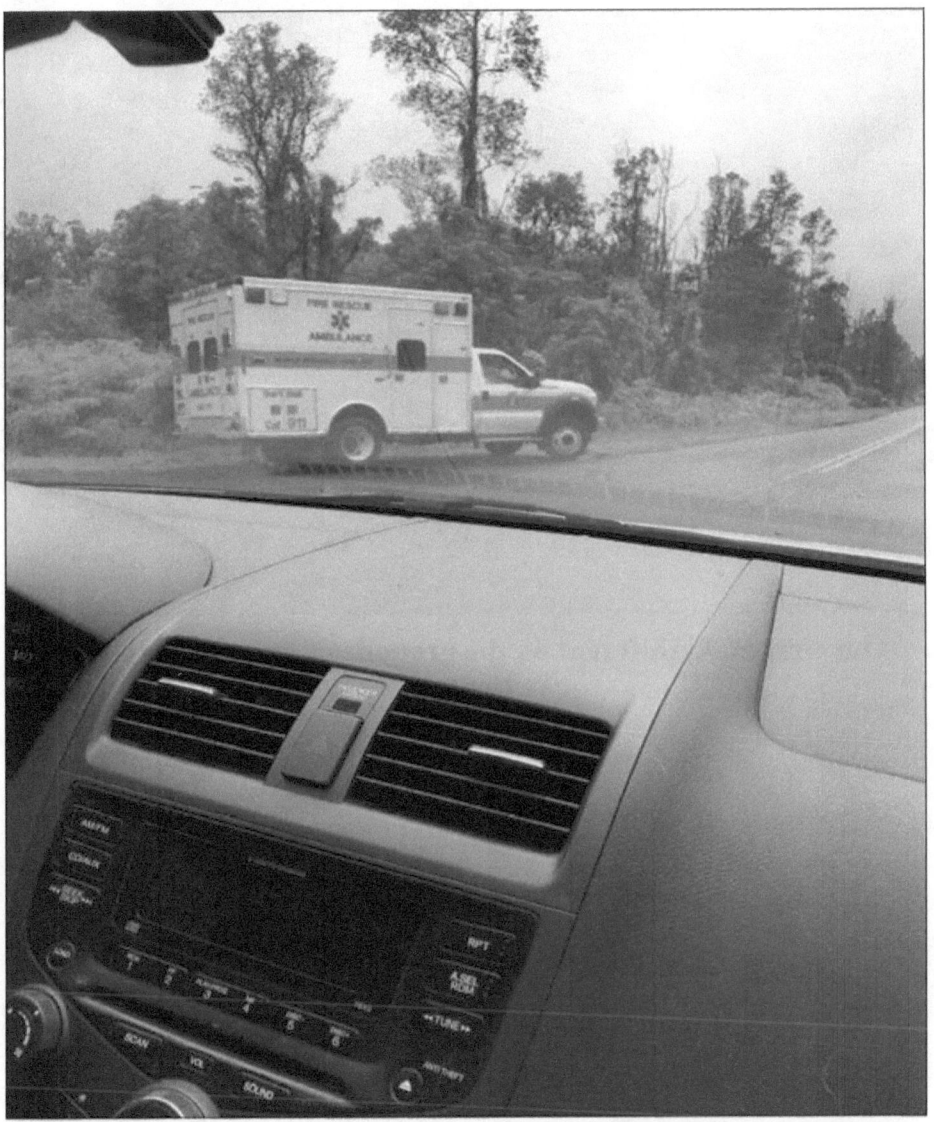

My car entered our subdivision during evacuation. Residents could obtain special clearance to enter disaster areas by Civil Defense. Emergency Ambulance was on standby at the entrance.

Our first makeshift tent on the grounds of Pahoa Community Center.

Inside tent feeder containers for our dog and two cats, kept with us during our ordeal.

The rescue helicopter hovering over our campsite was loud and noisy to evacuate residents trapped and unable to escape the lava surrounding their homes.

I captured a night photo with my camera, with red skies and smoke visible from burning homes, cars, trees, and dogs howling while we hunkered in our tents. Within the pavilion were cots, blankets, other provisions, hot meals by the Red Cross, local Churches, and residents from neighboring communities. The help came pouring in to aid the evacuees.

Tents lined up and scattered on the grounds of our local Community Center during evacuation.

At night, red skies with lights on Pahoa Community Center's grounds.

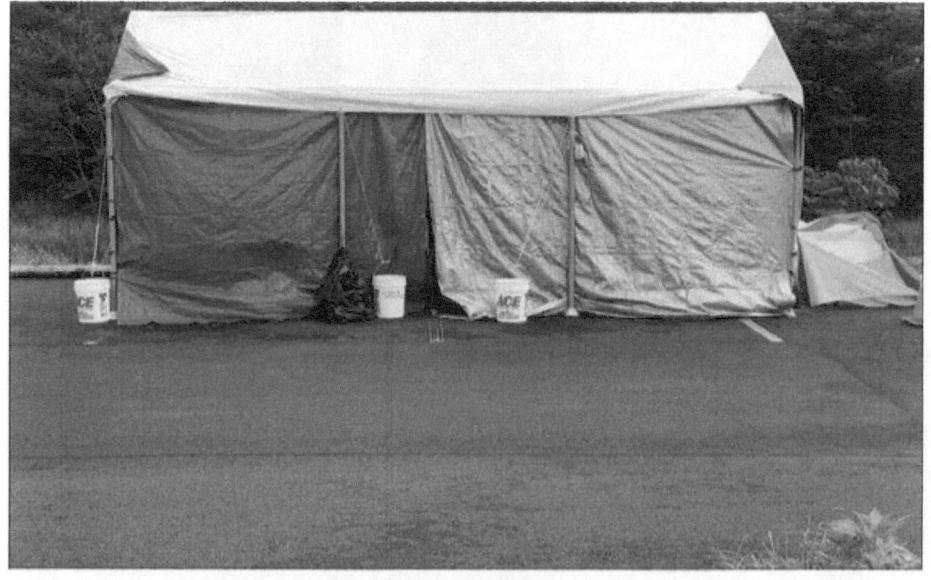

Picture of our upgraded living quarters.

The Hawaii National Guard was activated in our subdivision to protect homes from looters and measure hydrogen sulfide levels in the area for safe air levels.

A lava flow is visible crossing Leilani Ave, flowing further into other homes, subdivisions, and farms. It burned whatever was in its way, leaving a path of destruction and draining into the ocean.

Blockade of Leilani Ave by Civil Defense, lava flow slightly visible in the photo.

Our home was just five streets from Fissure 8 and suffered corrosion damage to all metal roofs, appliances, plumbing, etc., due to volcanic gases.

Residents were allowed back into their homes to gather whatever they needed in areas without activity. Before the eruption, earthquakes occurred within our subdivision. My husband, Bill, and I sought shelter at the Pahoa Community Center, where Red Cross services were available. The community support was fantastic, as was the support from Churches.

I clearly remember sleeping in my car when I heard a knock on my window. It was still morning, and a woman stood outside to get my attention. She had come from Kona, West Hawaii, with supplies provided by the community for the evacuees of Puna, East Hawaii, where the eruption occurred.

She offered to put up a tent for me and provided other supplies like an air mattress, a lantern, blankets, and other essentials. I watched from my car as she started getting things together. A Fire Department truck parked across from me and set up their tent to evaluate air quality for hydrogen sulfide gas because of the volcanic eruption. They came over to aid the woman who was setting up our tent. It was up and done in an instant. Our new home was ready for use on the pavement of the community center. Here was our first provision by the hand of God. Total strangers came to our aid. We lived with our dog and two cats in a tent. Meals were available three times a day—donations in a community store where we had free access. The Humane Society came in with provisions for the animals at the shelter. Showers were available at the community swimming pool.

The rain came pouring down, flooding the area. Water ran down the pavement like a river inches high, and wind and rain pelleted our humble tents. Animals were restless, barking and howling, and helicopters were above us as they tried to evacuate people who could not escape their homes. Skies were an eerie red with dark black smoke from burning houses, trees, foliage, automobiles, and other items.

Evacuees within the center got together to move canopies that were not in use, placing them over our soaked tents to keep us dry.

We were protected by unknown people in the darkness of night. Later, we discovered that the canopy covering our tent was from the Prayer Tent used by Christian church members during the day. Unknown to us, we had a prayer covering above us, which unknown fellow evacuees placed. Once more, I recognized the Mighty Hand of God protecting us.

My son, Michael, a Corrections Officer, had friends who offered to open their home for our use until we could return to our home in Leilani

Estates. Thank God for friends and the Lord who provided and protected us in our hours of crisis. The volcano spared our house, even though it was five streets away from Fissure 8, where molten lava flowed as it headed toward the ocean.

The corrosion damaged our roof, plumbing, appliances, and other items.

We applied for aid from FEMA, which was a wasted effort. We applied for assistance from our insurance company. They claimed no lava damage and would not cover us for corrosive damage. What were we to do?

Prayer, of course! We put our faith and trust in the Lord!

Months passed, and our home was severely damaged. We retired and were on a fixed income.

Months went by until I read an article in our local paper! A few residents in our area had taken the insurance company to court and won the case.

I felt hope, so I reapplied with the insurance company, which compensated me for damages.

Our house was restored to new condition and paid for with the insurance payout.

Thank You, Jesus. You are our provider, protector, and advocate!

CHAPTER 12
NEPAL BY DIVINE APPOINTMENT

The harvest is ripe and plentiful in this nation where there are very few Christians. Christianity is increasing; pastors are being trained, and churches and orphanages are running under the capable guidance of a Born-Again Spirit-filled minister who has a powerful testimony of how he was delivered out of the idol worship within the local population.

Due to COVID-19, the Christian Church in Nepal is losing local pastors who have been saved and trained for ministry outreach.

The Word preached new churches started, and the Bible was available.

Recently, a Pastor invited me to join the church in Nepal as they held their Sabbath Service online via Zoom. The online service gave me an opportunity to join fellow believers in Nepal and an excellent opportunity to speak to the church in Nepal by invitation of the pastor. COVID-19 has brought changes and new opportunities. God changed evil to good. Hallelujah and Amen!

My life continues to belong to Jesus, and I will continue to serve Him as long as I live or until He returns. It has been an exciting walk with Abba Father, Brother Jesus, and my Comforter and Advocate the Holy Spirit. I pray this testimony will reach and touch others in their walk with Jesus. Amen!

I do not know what the future here on earth has in store for me, but I do know someone who knows from Beginning to End; I can put my trust in Him—totally!

"And they overcame him by the blood of the Lamb, and by the word of their testimony, and they loved not their lives unto the death." Revelation 12:11 (KJV)

ABOUT THE AUTHOR

Rose P. Atkins's life is a testament to the unwavering love and grace of God. Her upcoming book, "Unconditional Love: God's Love for His Fallen Creatures", is a heartfelt journey through the trials and triumphs of a woman who has seen the hand of God in every chapter of her life.

Born in Honolulu, Hawaii, and raised in Kaneohe, Oahu, Rose witnessed the attack on Pearl Harbor as a child, an event that marked the beginning of a life filled with extraordinary experiences. From escaping an abusive marriage to participating in evangelistic crusades and outreach missions in Africa, Rose's story is one of resilience and faith. She even survived an erupting volcano, a testament to her enduring spirit and God's protective love.

Rose's professional journey is as remarkable as her personal one. She obtained her LPN License in Nursing from Kapiolani Community College and dedicated twenty-seven years to serving the hopeless and less fortunate. Her roles ranged from an office nurse in various specialties to a medication and treatment nurse in long-term care. She also served as a Federal employee in Occupational Health and spent nineteen years at Tripler Army Medical Hospital, working in Pediatrics, Women's Medical, and the Emergency Room.

Her passion for service extended beyond her professional life. Rose was ordained as a Stephen Minister and served as a Sunday School teacher, Superintendent, and outreach worker in prisons. She led Bible studies for youth and women's corrections and was actively involved in the 700 Club telephone and outreach ministry. Her dedication to helping others was recognized with an appointment to the Board of Substance Abuse and Mental Health by Governor Waihee.

Rose's life is a beautiful reflection of God's love and His desire to restore fallen humanity. Her story is a classic example of how God can transform a lost soul into a vessel fit for His use. Through her book, she hopes to inspire readers with her testimony of God's excellent, loving, fatherly guidance and intervention.

Now retired, Rose enjoys the simple pleasures of life. She finds solace in nature, the ocean, and gardening at her residence in Leilani Estates, Pahoa, Hawaii. Despite being widowed for two years, she finds comfort in her pets: Hekili, which means Thunder, and her two cats, Oreo and Hilo.

Rose P. Atkins's life is a masterpiece of God's handiwork, and her story is sure to inspire and uplift all who read it.